SHAKESPEARE RETOLD

THE TEMPEST

by

Martin Waddell & Alan Marks

W
FRANKLIN WATTS
LONDON•SYDNEY

First published in 2008
by Franklin Watts
338 Euston Road
London NW1 3BH

Franklin Watts Australia
45–51 Huntley Street
Alexandria
NSW 2015

Text copyright © Martin Waddell 2008
Illustrations copyright © Alan Marks 2008
Notes copyright © Franklin Watts 2008

Editor: Jackie Hamley
Designer: Peter Scoulding

A CIP catalogue record for this book is available from
the British Library.

ISBN: 978 0 7496 7744 2 (hbk)
ISBN: 978 0 7496 7750 3 (pbk)

Printed in China

Fnanklin Watts is a division of
Hachette Children's Books,
an Hachette Livre UK company.
www.hachettelivre.co.uk

CONTENTS

The Cast   4

Prologue   5

Shipwreck   6

Full Fathom Five   15

Two Murderous Plots   20

The Log Man   28

A Harpy's Screech   33

Epilogue   43

Notes   44

THE CAST

Prospero – a magician and the
rightful Duke of Milan
Miranda – Prospero's daughter
Ariel – a spirit of the air
Caliban – a half human monster

Antonio – Prospero's brother who has
seized the dukedom of Milan
Alonso – King of Naples
Ferdinand – Alonso's son and Prince of Naples
Sebastian – Alonso's brother

Gonzalo – wise counsellor to Alonso
Trinculo – Alonso's jester
Stefano – Alonso's drunken butler

The shipmaster, sailors and spirits

PROLOGUE

A magician raises a terrible storm. A monster
plots murder. Spirits taunt and sing. A feast
vanishes as a harpy screeches on an island
where no one and no thing is what it seems.

When the tempest roars on that beautiful
shore of strange visions and music ...

a world is rearranged.

CHAPTER ONE

SHIPWRECK

Duke Antonio of Milan and King Alonso of Naples were returning from the wedding of the king's daughter to a prince in faraway Africa.

As their ship drifted close to a beautiful and mysterious island the sky darkened suddenly.

Thunder roared, lightning flashed, rain lashed down as giant waves drove the ship toward the rocky coast.

Duke Antonio tried in vain to take command of the terrified sailors.

"If your Grace has the authority to give orders to the sea, do so!" the shipmaster roared. "If not, go to your cabin and prepare to die."

"I'd give a thousand furlongs of sea for an acre of land!" groaned Gonzalo, King Alonso's wise counsellor, as the waves broke over the ship.

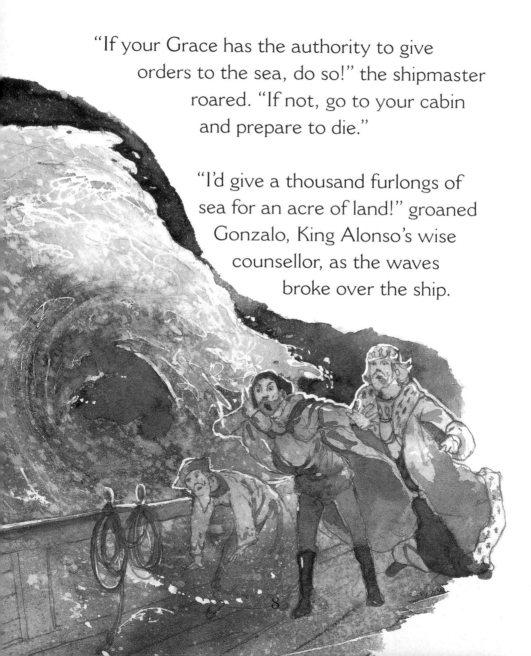

8

Two figures watched the grim scene from the shore. One was Prospero, a magician, the other his daughter, Miranda.

"If you have raised this storm, Father, stop it now!" the horrified girl sobbed.

"Take comfort, my daughter," Prospero calmed her. "I have arranged things so that not a hair of any man's head will be harmed."

The girl was still distressed.

"Tell me Miranda," said Prospero. "Do you remember the time before we came to this island, when you were an infant?"

"Didn't I have five women once, who looked after me?" the girl asked.

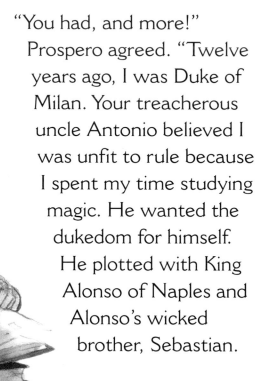

"You had, and more!" Prospero agreed. "Twelve years ago, I was Duke of Milan. Your treacherous uncle Antonio believed I was unfit to rule because I spent my time studying magic. He wanted the dukedom for himself. He plotted with King Alonso of Naples and Alonso's wicked brother, Sebastian.

I was overthrown and we were cast away in a boat without sails and left to die."

"How did we escape death?" the girl asked.

"The king's good counsellor Gonzalo showed mercy," Prospero replied. "He loaded the boat with food, water, clothes and my magical books ... we survived, and drifted to this island."

"But ..." started Miranda.

"I have told you enough," the magician said, raising his staff.

The girl fell
asleep instantly.
Prospero summoned
his servant Ariel, a
spirit of the air.

"I have done as you
commanded, master,"
Ariel told him. "The
ship did not sink. It
lies in a calm bay and
the sailors slumber
beneath the
hatches. All the
nobles are safe and
scattered round
the island."

"You must test
them to discover
their true natures,"
Prospero said.

"More work?" Ariel sighed. "I have been a faithful servant and you promised me my freedom."

"Remember the torment from which I freed you?" Prospero replied. "The witch Sycorax, who once ruled here, had imprisoned you in a tree because you refused to obey her wicked commands. It was my magic that released you after her death."

"I thank you for that master," Ariel said humbly. "I will obey!"

When Ariel had flown off to do his master's bidding, Prospero summoned Sycorax's son, Caliban, a half human monster who was his unwilling slave. Robbed by Prospero of the island he had inherited from his mother, Caliban hated the magician.

"May a south-west wind blow and blister you all over!" Caliban muttered. "You taught me to speak, to name the sun and moon. I loved you for it, and showed you the fresh springs and fertile places of my beautiful island. Cursed be I that did so, for now you keep me prisoner among the rocks."

"I treated you well at first," Prospero told him. "But you tried to attack my daughter. Now do as I command! Gather logs for my fire!"

The reluctant monster obeyed. He and Prospero had this in common: both had scores to settle.

Meanwhile ...

CHAPTER TWO

FULL FATHOM FIVE

... elsewhere on the island ...

King Alonso's son, Ferdinand, wandered through a magical landscape that seemed to change as he moved, so that he never quite knew where he was.

Believing
that his father
had drowned,
he was teased and
tormented by the
singing of the invisible Ariel.

"Full fathom five thy father lies,
  Of his bones are coral made.
Sea Nymphs hourly ring his bell,
    Ding-dong! Ding-dong!"

Ariel sang, testing the young man as
Prospero had instructed. Would Ferdinand
weep for his father, Alonso, or would he rejoice
that the throne of Naples would now be his?

The young man wept.

Ariel led him on toward the magician's cave.

"Open your eyes, Miranda!" Prospero
whispered, waking his daughter from her
enchanted sleep as Ferdinand
approached.

"I never saw anything so noble!"
the girl exclaimed.
"Is he a spirit like Ariel?"

"He is human," Prospero
assured her. "He eats
and sleeps and
feels like us."

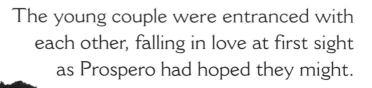

The young couple were entranced with each other, falling in love at first sight as Prospero had hoped they might.

"If you aren't married, I'll make you Queen of Naples!" Ferdinand said, gazing in wonder at Miranda.

The magician thrust himself between them, pretending anger.

"Traitor! You have come here to steal my island from me!" he roared at Ferdinand.

Ferdinand reached for his sword but found himself instantly enchanted, unable to move.

"Father, have pity," Miranda pleaded. "Why are you so rough with him? I have seen no gentler man than this."

"You have seen no other man than Caliban!"
Prospero smiled.

Ferdinand and Miranda's love was part of his
plan, but first he had to be sure that
Ferdinand was worthy of his daughter.

Meanwhile ...

CHAPTER THREE

TWO MURDEROUS PLOTS

… elsewhere on the island …

The royal party searched for survivors of the wreck, with King Alonso hoping that his son might have somehow escaped death.

They followed the sounds of strange music and whisperings through the magical maze of the enchanted island.

Stranger still, their robes had dried instantly when they struggled out of the sea, and looked just as magnificent as before.

"We can rejoice at our escape!" Gonzalo urged Alonso, but the king could think of nothing but the missing Ferdinand.

"What strange fish has made a meal of my son?" he groaned.

"If you hadn't married your daughter off so far from home, we would never have been on this fatal voyage," the king's brother Sebastian snapped sourly. "The fault is your own!"

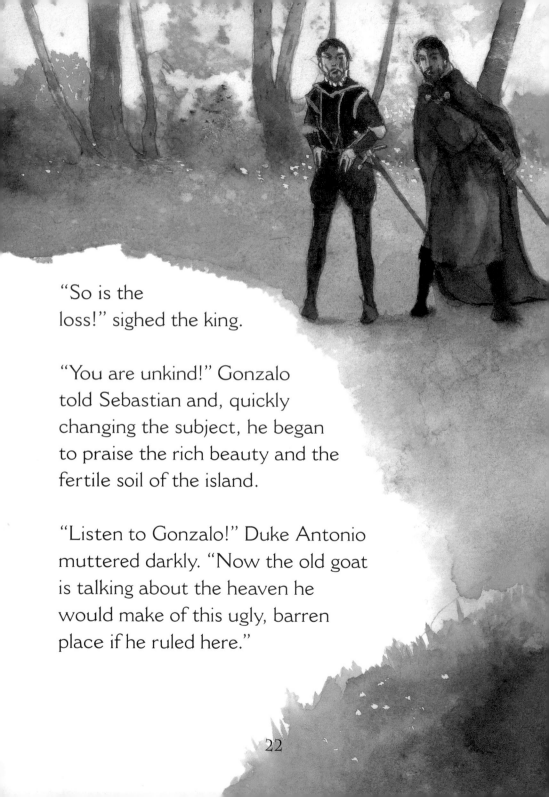

"So is the
loss!" sighed the king.

"You are unkind!" Gonzalo
told Sebastian and, quickly
changing the subject, he began
to praise the rich beauty and the
fertile soil of the island.

"Listen to Gonzalo!" Duke Antonio
muttered darkly. "Now the old goat
is talking about the heaven he
would make of this ugly, barren
place if he ruled here."

"Long live King Gonzalo!" Sebastian sneered.

Suddenly, as though a wizard had cast a spell
or some spirit an enchantment, all the royal
party fell asleep ... all but the wicked
Sebastian and the scheming Antonio.

"What strange sleep is this?"
Sebastian gasped, but Antonio
saw an opportunity
at once.

He had won the dukedom of Milan by an act of treachery against his brother. His friend Sebastian could win the throne of Naples in the same way.

"With the king's son in a watery grave and his daughter so far away, you inherit the throne if Alonso should die," he suggested. "Take your chance, as I did mine, and three inches of cold steel will make you King of Naples."

"I'll follow your example!" Sebastian agreed, and they advanced on the sleeping Alonso with their swords drawn.

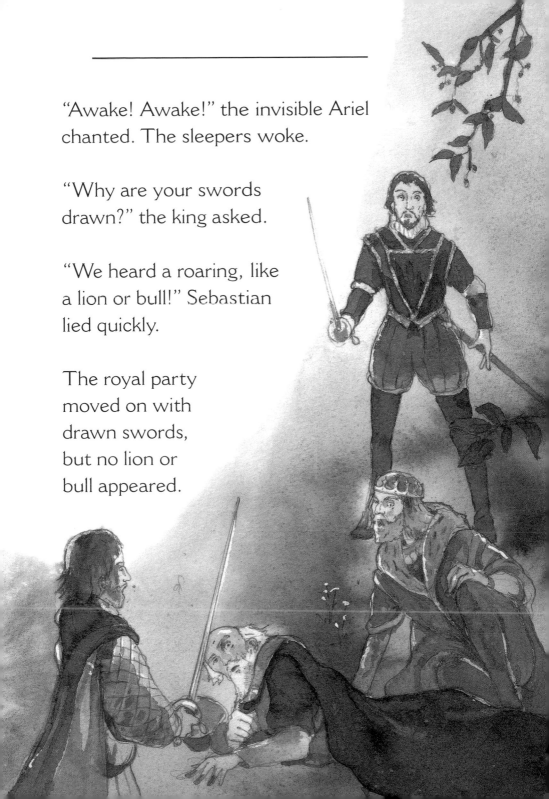

"Awake! Awake!" the invisible Ariel chanted. The sleepers woke.

"Why are your swords drawn?" the king asked.

"We heard a roaring, like a lion or bull!" Sebastian lied quickly.

The royal party moved on with drawn swords, but no lion or bull appeared.

As one murderous plot failed, so another was being planned. The monster Caliban came upon Trinculo and Stephano, the king's jester and butler, drinking wine stolen from the sinking ship.

Stephano's drunken boasting convinced the slow-witted monster that the butler was a god come down to earth.

"Kill Prospero, my lord!" Caliban pleaded, believing that his new god could rid him of the magician who had stolen his island. "Then you can rule here and marry his daughter."

"Is she a good-looking girl?" Stephano giggled, and Caliban nodded.

"Then monster, I'll kill Prospero!" Stephano promised. "His daughter and I will be king and queen of this island. You and Trinculo will be lords."

They set off to find Prospero ... but the unseen Ariel had heard every word.

Meanwhile ...

CHAPTER FOUR

THE LOG MAN

... elsewhere on the island ...

Ferdinand worked hard,
dragging heavy logs. Miranda
slipped out of the magician's cave,
not knowing that her father was watching.

"Rest a while," she begged Ferdinand.
"Let me carry the logs for you."

"I'd rather break my back than have you work while
I sit doing nothing," Ferdinand told her. "I wish only
to serve you. I am a patient log man for your sake."

"Do you love me?" she asked.

"I love and prize you beyond anything
else in the world," he replied.

"Then I'll be your servant, whether you wish it or not!" the girl smiled.

Satisfied by what he had heard, Prospero came out of hiding.

"If I have treated you badly, it was to test you," he told Ferdinand. "Sit now and talk with my daughter. You have my blessing!"

He made the island spirits sing their praises in a magical pageant.

"So rare and wise a father makes this place a paradise!" Ferdinand whispered to Miranda.

"Enough!" the magician frowned, remembering the plot which Ariel had overheard. He still had the monster Caliban to deal with. The spirits melted away, as though they had never existed.

"Your father seems upset!" Ferdinand whispered to Miranda.

"Don't be afraid of what you have seen," Prospero reassured them. "Like these spirits, we are such stuff as dreams are made of, and our little life is rounded with a sleep. This will pass but my brain is troubled. Go to the cave while I do what I have to do."

Alone again, Prospero summoned Ariel.

"Caliban and his friends come dripping mud from a swamp that I dumped them in," the spirit told him.

When the drunken would-be murderers arrived they found flashy clothes hung on a bush, cheap imitations of royal robes.

"See your majesty's new wardrobe, King Stephano!" Trinculo gurgled, and Caliban began to doubt his new god as the two drunkards played dressing up games with the clothes.

"Let's do the murder first!" the monster pleaded.

Prospero had seen and heard enough. With Ariel's help he unleashed the island spirits in the form of hunting dogs and the drunken men fled screaming.

"Hark how they roar!" Ariel mocked.

"You shall soon have your freedom," Prospero promised the spirit.

Meanwhile ...

CHAPTER FIVE

A HARPY'S SCREECH

... elsewhere on the island ...

The royal party wandered around the enchanted island, totally lost.

"This maze exhausts me," Gonzalo sighed. "I must rest."

"We'll search no more," King Alonso agreed wearily. "My son must be dead."

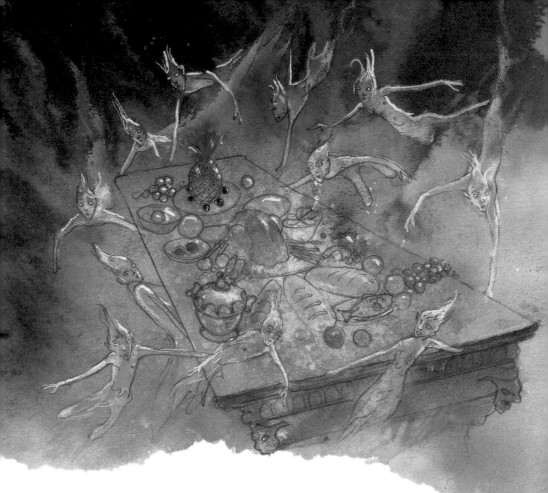

Suddenly weird music sounded
and, to their amazement, spirits of the
air appeared before them, bearing a table
heavily laden with food and drink.

"Now I believe in unicorns!" Sebastian
gasped, but his delight was shortlived. A clap
of thunder ... and the food disappeared.

In the same instant
Ariel appeared before
them as a harpy, a half
human creature with
sharp talons, a
human head and the
body of a vulture.

"You three men of sin!" the harpy screeched at
Alonso, Antonio and Sebastian. "The evil you did
Prospero has brought you to madness and
damnation on this island. You cast him to the sea,
and now that same sea and all the elements rage
against you. Nothing but sorrow awaits you here."

Thunder roared again, and the dreadful
vision vanished.

The men ran in fear, but Ariel led them
into a magic circle which Prospero
had drawn on the ground.
Once inside it, they were
unable to move a muscle.

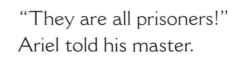

"They are all prisoners!"
Ariel told his master.

"Soon I will release them
and use this rough magic
no more," Prospero
said, breaking his magic
staff. "Then you shall
have your freedom, spirit!"

The magician came among the royal
party, invisibly at first, praising
Gonzalo for his wisdom and mercy,
and condemning the others for
their treachery. Then Prospero
revealed himself to them in his
ducal robes.

"Behold the wronged Duke
of Milan speaks to you!" he
said sternly.

Astonished by this unexpected
return from the grave of one they
thought dead, they cowered in
fear before him.

"Prospero alive? As King of
Naples I restore the dukedom
of Milan to you!" Alonso
quivered. "And I humbly
beg your forgiveness."

"I forgive you," said
Prospero, embracing
the king. Then he
embraced old
Gonzalo, saying,
"You saved my
life, and my
daughter's.
I give you
thanks."

"You too I forgive!" he told his traitorous brother Antonio and the wicked Sebastian, adding in a whisper: "*At this time* I will tell no tales of how you plotted to kill Alonso." The unmistakable threat that lay behind his words stunned them into silence.

"How come you to this place, where I lost my son three short hours ago in a storm?" Alonso broke in.

"I too lost my daughter in that storm," Prospero replied, appearing downcast.

"Oh that they were alive!" groaned Alonso.

"I'll show you something now that will make you as content as I am with my dukedom," Prospero smiled, pulling back a curtain in his cave to reveal Ferdinand and Miranda.

"If this is but another of your island visions, Prospero, I'll lose my son twice!" Alonso gasped.

Then Ferdinand spoke to his father. "Sir, here is my chosen wife!"

"Oh brave new world that has such people in it!" Miranda exclaimed, seeing the magnificently dressed nobles for the first time.

"It's new to thee!" Prospero muttered.

"Blessings to you both, and forgive me for what I did to your father," Alonso told the girl.

With that the ship's crew appeared, brought by Ariel. Soon they would all sail home.

Ariel, free at last, would fly no one knew where.

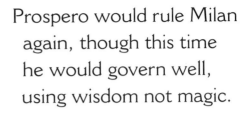

Prospero would rule Milan again, though this time he would govern well, using wisdom not magic.

The treacherous Antonio and Sebastian posed no more threat, gripped by the fear that Prospero could reveal their murderous plan to Alonso if he chose to.

The marriage of Ferdinand and Miranda made a happy union between Milan and Naples ... a brave new world indeed.

Meanwhile ...

… on the island …

Caliban lived on in that place of mad dreams,
that savage, mystical, magical place, where he
was as he wanted to be …

… master of his strange island.

EPILOGUE

A magician raised a terrible storm. A monster plotted murder. Spirits taunted and sang. A feast vanished with a harpy's screech on an island where no one and no thing was quite what it seemed.

When the tempest roared on that beautiful shore of strange visions and music ...

a world was rearranged.

NOTES

by Dr Catherine Alexander

In 1609, four hundred people set sail from England for a new life in America. The convoy hit a violent storm and the Governor's ship, the *Sea Venture*, was blown off course. The ship was separated from the others and landed on the island of Bermuda. The survivors built two new ships and eventually made it safely to Jamestown the following year. News of the shipwreck reached England, and this gave Shakespeare ideas for writing his play, *The Tempest*.

The early seventeenth century was an age of exploration and discovery for brave travellers. What lands might be found? Who might live there? There were rumours of monsters and

cannibals. Shakespeare
invented two very unusual
characters to inhabit the
island in his play: Caliban
(whose name is very close
to 'cannibal') and Ariel.

Who or what can they be and
what might they look like? When
the play was first published in
1623 the cast list described
Caliban as 'a salvage and deformed
slave' and Ariel as 'an airy spirit'.
Neither is easy to portray on stage.

Caliban, the role that was the play's leading part in
the nineteenth century, has been played as a
savage human eating raw fish, as different animals
including a tortoise, as half human and half animal
covered in fur and crawling on the ground, and as
a slave in chains. He has been shown as a victim,
bullied by Prospero, and as a villain who tries to
attack Miranda.

Ariel was played first by a boy in Shakespeare's theatre company but for many years afterwards was a role for an actress, often dressed as a fairy with wings.

Both Caliban and Ariel have been played by black actors and have made Prospero look like a wicked slave owner. Often, however, Prospero is presented sympathetically and sometimes presented as if he is Shakespeare himself.

Although Shakespeare went on to write jointly with other playwrights, *The Tempest* is the last play that he wrote on his own, probably in 1611. Many have seen Prospero's great speeches, particularly when he speaks of breaking his magic staff and drowning his magic book, as Shakespeare announcing that he will not write his magical and exciting plays any more, and will retire from the hectic world of the London theatre and return to his home town of Stratford upon Avon.

The first record of a performance of *The Tempest* was for the court at Whitehall, one of King James' palaces in London, in November 1611. James was the patron of Shakespeare's theatre company (which is why they were called the King's Men) and Shakespeare, who was an actor as well as a playwright, often performed for the royal family.

The Tempest had a second royal performance in 1613 to celebrate the wedding of James' daughter, Princess Elizabeth. Court productions could be lavish affairs, using architects, artists, designers, engineers, musicians, gymnasts and dancers to create spectacular special effects, sets and costumes that were not possible in the public theatres.

Court shows, called masques, could have wave machines and revolving scenery so the magic of *The Tempest* would have been exciting to watch.

THE TEMPEST FACTS

❖ Some of the greatest actors have played Prospero including Derek Jacobi and Patrick Stewart. John Gielgud's beautiful voice made him a famous Prospero and he appeared in a film version of the play, called *Prospero's Books*, as well as performing it on stage many times.

❖ Shakespeare's plays usually have a range of settings and stories that cover many years. *The Tempest* is unique because the action occurs in one place – the island – and in one day.

❖ The magical characters in *The Tempest* have fascinated artists from the eighteenth century onwards and Caliban, Ariel and Prospero have been painted and drawn many different ways. How do you think they should look?